THE FORMER LIVES
OF SAINTS

(some) other Books By EMP

Trail Her Trash
by Lola Nation

my lungs are a dive bar
by Walter Moore

Soulslut
by mooshe

Parade of Malfeasance
by Joseph Goosey

Test Swan
by J.I.B. & Gavin McGuire

Beautiful Earthworms & Abominable Stars
by Jeanette Powers & Ezhno Martin

those who favor fire, those who pray to fire
by Ben Brindise & Justin Karcher

This One's ~~For~~ Me
by Ellen Lutnick

Ten-Foot-Tall-And-Bulletproof
by Jason Ryberg

THE FORMER LIVES OF SAINTS

Poems

Damian Rucci &
Ezhno Martín

Columbus, Ohio
empbooks.com

Copyright © 2017 by Damian Rucci and Ezhno Martín

We find discussions of our rights — as publishers and authors — to be laughable, all things considered. Please claim this work as your own. Please republish it and sell it on street corners. Please include our material in ALL of your get-rich-quick schemes. All we ask is that you accept responsibility for any libel lawsuits.
Speaking of which ...
This book is a *complete* work of fiction. Names, characters, places, opinions, dreams, dates, impressions, monologues about a certain New York City basketball team, emotional trauma, statistics, and predictions are products of the author's imagination and/or are symptoms of mental illness. We are not in the business of accepting responsibility for anything and will deny we actually made this book and blame Tom Thibodeau at every turn.

A Better Edition:10 19 33 34 6 11 1973
ISBN: 978-0-9985077-2-9
LOC: 2017938985

Design, Layout, and Cover Art: Ezhno Martín
Edits: Ezhno Martín, Damian Rucci, Jeanette Powers

Damian Rucci

Corners & Eternity   / 1
Gospel   / 3
All The Junkies On Carr Avenue   / 4
Antares   / 6
Y'all Were Just the Pregame   / 7
Garden State Slammer   / 9
Is The Next Stop Chicago or Heaven?   / 10
Sons of Twilight   / 11
A Poet's Prayer   / 12
Bathroom Stalls   / 14
Bad Shepherds   / 16
When Smoking Dope in a Hotel Room   / 18
Burn Out   / 19
Softcore Porn Never Sounded Like This   / 20
Winter Moon   / 22
BLACK LIGHTNING   / 23
Note from the Underground   / 24
Blunt Guts   / 25
Us & Roses   / 26
Complimentary Stationary   /28
Everyone is Wearing Masks and It's Not Even Halloween   / 29
Blacktop Beatitudes   / 30
Late Night Sutra   / 31
This Illness   / 32
Little Miss Melancholy & The Left Hand Path   / 33
Summerland   / 35
Poets Like Us   / 36

Ezhno Martín

Liberated (Lady-Clothes) / 43
11.5.86 / 47
32-Ounce Gatorade Bottles Are A Lady-Man's Best Friend / 51
You SNEAKY Bitch / 53
Sit On My Face Soulmate / 55
Professional Failure / 59
In Junk Yard Dogs We Trust / 61
Dead Flowers in Denial / 63
Long Island Sound / 65
Shit-Brains Soup / 69
If Love / 72
Only In Dreams Wet With Ferlinghetti's Sweat / 74
Shining Time Space-Station / 76
I Guess I'll Never Learn / 79
Big Strong Man / 82
Drunk Driving Is NOT An Extreme Sport / 84
A Love Poem Not Quite About Jason Ryberg / 88
Murphy's Eulogy: As Dictated / 90
Powers Whiskey / 91

*...if they could build houses
out of regrets
we'd all live in castles...*

Damian Rucci

is a writer and poet from New Jersey whose work has recently appeared in Eunoia Review, Beatdom, Lehigh Valley Vanguard, and Rising Phoenix Review. He is the author of Tweet and Other Poems (Maverick Duck Press 2016) and Symphony of Crows (Indigent Press 2015) and the founder and host of the Poetry in the Port Reading Series. Someday, he might even be the Poet Laureate of Gas Station Bathrooms and Hillbilly Hot tubs.

Corners & Eternity

These fingers
have been scribbling this week
and I'm not sure
what drives them to do so

but I know that some nights
I want to be remembered
after this crazy ride
as another paragraph
in literature's anthology
if they're still printing that
on paper in the future

Some nights I want
back streets in bohemian cities
to carry my name
and at night when the fourteen-year-olds smoke
their parent's cigarettes on the corners
I want them to wonder
what I would have been like
to know me

Some nights I want beat souls
to read my words and chew on them
like day old french bread
as they sift through another
empty night with a beer
and untied work boots

But these words probably
won't do that

I'd toss them in the trashcan
by the corner of my desk
but I'm writing this on my phone

Some nights
I admire the beauty of absence
like how the still of twilight
gives way to daybreak
and we never mourn the star covered skies
we just admire them
while they hang above our heads
and forget about them
as the sun rises

Gospel-

When the sun is hot
and the sky is blue
I remember the summers
of my youth
kicking rocks down the
Henry Hudson trail.

The lost souls drinking
beer in the Bayshore sun
teach lessons under
the lonely moon.

Where are those holy men
who showed us life
from the bottom
of bottles of Old English?

The patron saints of excess
are absent now —
their souls scrubbed from
the asphalt trails leaving
only echoes of their
gospel.

All The Junkies on Carr Avenue

look a lot like us in the yellow street lights
that paint their silhouettes in flickers

skeletons

in dirty denim dance
behind burning red embers
they're dead before the next needle hits their

flesh

what happened to what's-his-name?
Or the one after that or you
with your baby blue eyes
how did we become this?

We broke the vows of the block

we would never sniff powder
never chew pills
never charm the veins to the surface
by tying off a band of rubber
a syringe in the arm is death
without a certificate

Nothing stays the same

children

steal cigarettes and puke on warm beer

weed smoking beauty queens trade
innocence for hallway ecstasy
the artists dilute their genius until
their souls are vacant

We are doomed to be like our fathers
to be burnouts who die unknown

we are doomed to step over the bodies
of our

friends

Antares

It could just be the drugs
but I think we found innocence
tonight in the parking lot
in front of your house
watching the Antares Rocket
from your phone become a shooting star
across the Jersey sky
we waived to the spaceship
becoming alien in the Cassiopeia
of autumn lights.
I think of my youth, chasing daylight
along the beaches of the Bayshore
your smile reminds me of then
and I think maybe home
isn't a place but a series of moments
when you feel less alone

Y'all Were Just the Pregame

Some say life is like a river
& we're floating from the womb
to our caskets & you always try to hold on
but we all drift away from each other
so it's best to sit on your hands &
watch the world pass you by —
watch the breeze greet grasses
you'll never step on, watch the gulls
dance in cryptic seafoam winds

& some say life is like a race car
& nirvana can only be found with
the wind on your face, with a stampede
beneath your sternum, gulps of breath
are milestones to completion
life can end in a second & any second
without the thunder of release is too long
that the devil will get his due
once you get your hands on yours

but some say life is what you make of it,
that men should build monuments
out of their bones, to stack boulders
on their shoulders until they break the heavens
another obelisk smited by our limitations
& we all fall short & we all die
just a little more alone

I want the last taste of my tongue
to be the bitter lightning of adrenaline
to have the hair on my arms marching

to the drum of my screaming heart
to feel the wind beat my hollow bones
like it was the chorus of cherub angels

You'll know y'all were just the pregame
& that life ends one second at a time
& any second that takes me,
just know that I deserved it.

Garden State Slammer

The only rhythm in my chest
comes from the bass
of the black car beside me
in the parking lot
of McDonald's.

I'm so bored I could die.
So I'll smoke some more marijuana
day dream of hotel rooms in Toledo,
car rides down route 66 with
the mid-western breeze
on my balding scalp

There has to be something better
than the sea foam of the Atlantic
with her social security lullabies,
Beer chugging union workers
toast the Garden State to sleep
with sand in their boots
and decimal points in their heads.

America's armpit wants me to trade
the muse for a white jacket and a knife.
Cutting meat is a respected profession:
seventy thousand in blood money
is enough to start a life,
enough to buy a ring,
raise a couple of kids,
pay off that credit card debt
and die

Is The Next Stop Chicago, or Heaven?

On the corner of West 39th and Bell,
below the amber street light by the bookstore
I see you, Victor Smith,
reading beneath the moon.

We walk down Roanoke Rd
as you read me your poems —
I've never heard your voice but tonight
it is made of silk and bourbon.
Victor Smith, why have you come back here?
Why are you a vision in this late night stupor?
Where does the Midwest wind blow?
To Chicago
or to heaven?

How many street poets
know the devil by name?
I know, you've never claimed to be a teacher,
but tonight your words are gospel.
Victor, can dog-faced saints know serenity?
How many junkies have sold their last stanza
for a glimpse at the sun?
How many vagabonds have hopped trains
through cowtowns and became preachers
under their bridges?

How many cold lonely nights make a prophet?

Why do they always die alone?

Sons of Twilight

Between the hours of eleven at night
and eight in the morning
I aint no poet
I am a third shift worker,
I am a nine digit punch code,
I am another lost soul biding time
at a suburban grocery store.
But sometimes I feel it's worth
feeling good about.
The food for the neighborhood
doesn't just appear on the shelf,
it's put there by the sons of twilight;
the time biders; the drop outs; the dreamers;
the hungry.

A Poet's Prayer

There on West Front Street
where the bay crafts us a pearl
from the setting sun

silhouettes dance dusk away
smartphone bohemians
talk poetry behind cigarette smoke

Thursday is our sabbath
deep in the jowls of suburbia
we pray, we pray, we burn

I eat a handful of kratom
pull, pass a J to Burroughs
sobriety is a pipe dream
for men like us

but the reading goes on
Hupert steals the breath
from our lungs
replaces it with helium

we rise out of our bodies
become floating constellations
and crash to the Earth
as Burroughs drives us home

we pray, we pray, we burn

as we spill out
onto the sidewalks

baptized and renewed
we know it won't last

all of my angels
are on vacation
you know, it's time for trouble
so I say a poet's prayer

lord, keep the beer flowing
lord, keep the night going
lord, home ain't a place
but a series of moments
lord, keep the money
lord, keep the fame
but save me these friends
let these memories remain

Bathroom Stalls

Here we are again
Borza is breaking up
the pills on the sink
I'm watching the door
it's our nightly dance
it makes the world shine

It's always something
to make the night glow
always the adderall
always the ritalin
always the molly
and the weed keeps us grounded
keeps our hearts in our chests

Borza and I can't get off
the couch in the day but at night
we're entrepreneurs, we make it work
we're scientists— 400 mg of caffeine
is enough to double an addy 20
add a pack of smokes and you have
nirvana baby

we live for the lightning
howl into the empty 3am dawn
sit Buddha face as the sun greets suburbia
work isn't work when you're flying
work ain't just work when you're dying

we talk about all the things
we want to do on the outside

save money one day and clean up
but we both know we'll be
in that bathroom stall
again
tonight

We both know
there isn't anything on the outside
for men like us

Bad Shepherds

At 3am
Youth of a Nation
broke across the radio at work

but instead of Sandoval's
rapping over the treble of high hats
and bass guitar
your voice came through the speakers

You sang drunken out of tune
in the cool glow
of a supermarket twilight.

Cory,
Where has the time gone?
Day drinking malt liquor
while the sun burned horizon
into the blue of the bay.

We cut wakes into
the asphalt seas of the wilted garden state
singing to old songs
until our throats strained.

Cory,
Which way does your spirit blow?
Through the turnpike tundras
of Manalapan?
Does it hide beneath your bed
in Fulton Place where you hid marijuana
in a Pringle can?

I think it rides the breeze
over the wooden pilings
at the waterfront.
The rebellious air in the lungs
of the youth that took our place
breathing Atlantic and cursing sky.

Cory,
Do you know how much you meant to us?
You were the only good heart
out of the entire crew of misfits.
Your smile calmed our fists.
Your words paused our malice.

You were our
Newport smoking messiah
in a North Face vest
and you died so our sins
could become lessons.

You are the last breath
of an October moon
the warm glow
after a shot of whiskey.
The ache of longing
that pulses in our chests.

And tonight I thought
for a moment
you were alive again.

When Smoking Dope in a Hotel Room

Place a towel along the doorjamb

turn the shower up as hot as possible

wait until the steam hits the air

and toke.

hold the sweet smoke in your lungs,

wipe your tears from your eyes,

yesterday is gone.

try and laugh,

today is ending.

tomorrow we will have a home.

Burn Out

After sex
we looked from the fourth floor
condo windows out onto
the white beaches of the Jersey Shore
still naked, the sun on your breasts
you looked at me and said

I don't think you love me anymore

I said I did.

But how could I have said anything else?

We were young flames
on an empty beach in July
and to me then,
the fires we had were love

I hadn't watched the world burn
long enough to know any better
or even the words to
break it to you
if I did

Softcore Porn Never Sounded Like This

I haven't had phone sex since 2005
when Kay stopped calling me
from Canada.

She was three times
my age but she didn't care —
she was going to come
to the States and make
a man out of me

once the chemo
stopped and she could
walk again.

Kay said men her age
wouldn't give a woman
in a wheelchair a chance

while boys and girls
were coupling up
in dim-lit gymnasiums
swaying to hits from the 80s

I was stroking
my half limp prick
to her purring to me
things I didn't understand
and now can't remember

clenching my eyes shut
trying to conjure images
of what a vagina could look like
because the soft-core porn
commercials on channel 69
didn't show anything below the waist.

Like a drunken buffalo
I would thrash around my sheets
with my member in my hand
dancing along her words
with each slap of hand
on flesh

and when we would finish
I would slap my knees together
drunk off a cocktail of regret,
shame, and exhilaration,
say goodbye to Kay from Canada,
pull my waistband over my navel,
and slide down to the floor
so I could play with my action figures
before bedtime.

Winter Moon

Winter moon,
hiding in a bed of clouds
how many nights have you witnessed?
High in the chasm of twilight
a conduit of mother sun
who makes you shine your light?

Are you the proctor of the waves?
The glow of three am sutras
the ambience of the car jackers
on Broad Street?

Are you the ancient father
caressing gaia through the long nights?
Or the antithesis of sunshine
the velvet hue of sin
the machinery of our own corrosion?

Winter moon,
why do I only see you
when it feels like I am dying?

BLACK LIGHTNING

Isaiah's dad liked to drink and drive
before they took his license away
and those doctors cut off three toes.

Now he limps when he isn't on his bike.
A far cry from black lightning that would
peel out around the trailer park burning
tire treads into the asphalt.

I was eight then on my two wheeler,
admiring the way the wind broke
from the hood of his Volkswagen
as he swerved up & down the block
one hand on the steering wheel,

the wind on his beard.
The sun never set in his eyes and he grabbed
the daylight between each sip of Old English.

Now he pedals to the bar, Stryker's
that used to be Ted's when he was king.

Note from the Underground

we are the afterglow —
captured echoes with sun tans
day drunk apocalyptos
peddling art for memories
we are the last burning cigarette
of modern day inconvenience
and we're almost at the filter.

Blunt Guts

When the table is covered
in plastic bags
and the pink aluminum
of cigarillo packages.

Where the sweet stench
of yesterday's Chinese take out
still clings to the basement air

and the ash trays are full
of old roaches you'll smoke one day
when your money is tight
but the outside sky is still gray

the floors are catch-alls
for blunt guts and old match sticks

we'll remember those nights —
howling until dawn
playing the fiddles of apathy
as the outside world burns

Sometimes it's time to make things
sometimes it's time to do things
but sometimes stupor
is the only sense left in the world

Us & Roses

There is an empty
gallon of water
we fashioned into a vase

on the table

within it
a bouquet of dead roses
hang their burgundy pedals
in shame

as if knowing
they didn't try enough
to silence the screaming matches
that season our nights
with broken hearts
and regrets

the vase
and its wilted flowers
on the table
get buried with old take out

we may never see it again

we're too busy
dying in this one room bungalow
counting spare change
for dollar store burritos
enough gas to get to work
enough grass to numb the hurt

roses
sweet roses
if I buy another bouquet
will you save this relationship

will your blood red bloom
new hope within our chests

will your beauty make us forget
about the money we don't have
or the jobs we can't find
or the world we hide away from

but you will be there too
in a jug of water on a messy table
shrouded in darkness
dying while we destroy ourselves

I feel for you

the only time we see light either
is when we're punching
holes through walls
letting light beams touch
our pale skin

it's not so bad really

it's cheaper than a lamp

Complimentary Stationary

back in a hotel again
on another rainy weekend
we've done this dance before
we've written our wishes
on complimentary stationary

we've lived off free breakfast platters
murky instant coffee
and left over marijuana
it's always like this

the prophets twisted the truth
there is no honor in this
there is no pride in running away
Jack Kerouac always had a place
that he could return to

we wonder from heartbreak
to tragedy trying to pluck
poems from the wreckage
but we never find home
as a place, only as a feeling

when we're left with nothing
again but your head on my
shoulder feels quite nice
and I don't mind having nothing
if I have your kisses on my neck

Everyone is Wearing Masks and It's Not Even Halloween

it's later than that now, the leaves
have fallen across idle and empty streets
smiles are now forbidden fruits
eyes, the last bastion of contact
I never knew how much
I used to read lips

my brother has been reading lips
since 1996, the world a muffled
boombox on the edge of the cosmos
a floating mural of yearning
I know beauty still lingers
on the edge of quiet contemplations

all the coffee shops are closed
all the parties are over
the world is hushed like a first snow
my footsteps echo alone on Myrtle avenue
there is nothing normal about this newness
but there is no resolve but to submit

The Blacktop Beatitudes

I've finally learned
how to surrender
It's like riding a
two wheeler —
at first you fight
against your own balance
throwing yourself onto the asphalt
until your hands and knees
are bloody remnants
but then when you find it
it's like coasting on
a wide suburban street
in July when you are six
The warmth on your face
couples with the vibrations
of smooth blacktop
and in that moment
you know peace

Late Night Sutra

I sold my soul
to a grocery store
for eleven dollars an hour
and it doesn't look
like I'll be going anywhere
anytime soon
'cause nowhere else
pays so good
I only gotta work
seven days a week
ten hours a day
and they don't care
if I smoke dope
as long as the job is done
The world sleeps
while third shift chews
at my flesh like a plague
I can't even work sober
anymore
When will the sun rise?
how many more days in autumn?
how many more nights
chasing my youth
through these frozen food aisles
praying dawn brings
release?

This Illness

I watch the cars
up and town Broadway
across from Cag's bicycles
I wonder how many drive
idle with heavy hearts?

How many drift aimless
home from work with
grease burned into their arms
with tears scarred into the
corners of their eyes?

You can scrub the dirt from
your skin but you can't clean
this illness from your bones.

I am sick and she is sick
and we were born into this sick world.
The medicine men on the corners
hold our dreams and aspirations,

we've traded Californian vistas
and white fences for landscapes
of death and urban rot.

Tonight I say I am going to kill myself
I've said this every night for months
and with each haunted evening
I tiptoe closer to oblivion
with the faith of a preacher.

Little Miss Melancholy &
The Left Hand Path

to get to the muse, you have to get over the mood
& nothing is ever easy baby, we're not pretty
enough to catch the light of any morning star
the only breeze that whispers behind our ears
are sinister callings of the machinery of our
undoing

& death is the only thing that bonds us together:
that every late night has a painful haunted dawn
that every line of dopamine hides a tear-wet cheek
that every adventure brings us back with no money
that every friend will wander away a stranger
& it's always just been this way, you know?

we traded your mother's religion for mana & sin
found a new pantheon of gods & heroes haunting
midwestern streets hitching rides
through damnation
they too will die young & we will turn them
into martyrs
invoke their names & build legends
from their bones

Maybe there is magick coursing
through these veins
& the sigils along the floors
are dutch guts & silver
& we'll find gnosis at three in the morning
naked and pretty as if we've never known the sun
& that the death of this night will never come

We're less than angels & more than beasts
& I've never seen the gods but I've heard them
sing to me at night, but the light is piercing the
veil now & we've both run out of things to say

if God was real, he would pull her off of the floor
if God was real, we'd probably still be here right now
making these bones dance & riding lightning
when you're born to die
love alone is not enough to save you

Summerland

We said we would leave Jersey
by any means necessary; see the world
break out from the constructs
that made everyone boring

at first we started bands
played bad music hoping
to escape and when that didn't happen
we figured after high school we'd just bounce

but it never happened
the world moved onward, you cleaned up
while I found new faults in my character
life is slippery if you try and hold on

now you are a father
a little girl on your hip
you found manhood in an instant
you found a way to save your soul

while you are breaking your ass
for your own, I am writing poems
I have seven cents in my pocket
I have no idea what I'll do next

I found Summerland
in a quiet town in Nowhere Kingdom
I have no idea how I'll get home
I don't care what I'll do next.

Poets Like Us

I.

There are poets, whose poems
are written on dollar bills
whose parents bought them a degree in Iowa
whose good looks fill workshops in Manhattan

there are poets like us who chase America —
whose poems are written from dirty fingers
who smoke dope on the roofs of bars
counting the hundreds of Missouri stars
who chase down despair with cheap beer
and laughter

who carve the American highways
with tire treads
who read to basement dwellers
in small town Kansas
who breath American, not football on Sundays
American, not bombs in the Middle East
American, not trail of tears
American, but the America
that Whitman breathed, that Emerson,
that Twain, that Dickinson, that Angelou —
the America that Kerouac searched for

there are poets who die forgotten
whose words become symphonies in the wind
whose heartbeats become our rhythm
whose books sit on shelves waiting
for lost poets to find them

who's spirits become our ethos
whose names we can't remember

and this is the future we share
even Neil Cassidy died alone
on those railroad tracks

II.

Along the highways of mother America
hidden from the cool glow of strip mall America
shunned from the university America
there are poets who read poems to strangers
& friends & other lost souls
& those nights are dirty & holy & inspiring
& the street poets search for the truth
between each line of poetry sung
into the microphone bled into the page
their doctrines are in the manifestos
of the gas station bathroom walls
the soul graffiti of the wayward
bastards drifting west past the Mississippi
in pursuit of cheap rent and peace
with nothing but hope in their bellies
& words in their head

Somewhere in Blue Springs Missouri
Jason Baldinger tells me it's about the road
the books will sell
& sometimes they don't sell
but it's about the adventure between the stops
the drives through Kansas blasting Jazz
the faces along the back roads of America

it's about the poetry you can find out there
the poetry that needs to be found

III.

Outside of a Waffle House on the highway
Shawn Pavey reads us a poem
about Waffle House
& we laugh in the parking lot
smiling as the lone moon
grows full above the clouds
we wave goodbye too soon
the adventure is over by the morning
we will head back to our homes & our jobs
but the road will keep on moving
the sun will rise and set
behind strange landscapes
there are easier paths in this life
there are jobs that trade the human spirit
for credit cards & jewels
but the street poet is born to be outside of it all
born to take to the streets with poems in hand
born to follow the vagabond sunset to its coast

& I can feel this in my bones

Damian Rucci's Confirmation Name:
Genesius (Of Rome)

     Genesius was an everyday man who used comedy, poetry, and performance to mock the conventions of monolithic religion and Roman government. When he found a new truth, the Emperor tried to force him to renounce it but he gave the sacrifice of life as a final act of rebellion against the authoritarian rule. Genesius was a walking act of defiance. A man who did as he pleased. A man who died as he wanted and gave a final *FUCK YOU* to the evils of authoritarianism.

Genesius was the Patron Saint of Actors & Comedians

MÁS AMOR POR FAVOR

Ezhno Martín

is a (former) Kansas City Queer hearing the call of multiple former eastward homelands. Ezhno doesn't believe in pronouns and doesn't use them, but does believe in making books and tangible pieces of art to take home and love. Ezhno's *EMP* focuses on publishing freaks and females, but will publish dudes down with duende. Ezhno used to have a cat named Furlinghetti, but the cat found Ezhno tedious and stopped showing up for dinner. Ezhno hates self promotion, but you should buy a lot of books whenever possible. Better yet, read them to each other. Better yet, kiss your books. That is likely the only love Ezhno will be willing to accept.

Liberated (Lady-Clothes)

I was just sorting my mismatched laundry
                which is a mundane chore
      for someone who had long taken
no pride or pleasure in the clothes they wore
when a long black dress showed up
      at the bottom of the pile
            and I was wearing it before
I had a chance to wonder why

            It felt good
                    good like FINALLY
      it felt so good to finally see
a sexy reflection of myself in the mirror
            so I doubled down
      and stole my girlfriend's lipstick
I'd been wearing eyeliner for years
      but had never made the connection
            that I was
    I guess
                  secretly some kind of queer

        I'd been wearing
      only the blander shades of grey
because I'd never felt worth more
        but suddenly a new smile
              stared back at me
and glistening red lips told me I was a peacock
      a song bird on the first day of spring
and I was actually excited to go shopping
          and try on clothes
      like I couldn't wait to wear them

I couldn't wait to show the world
my sultry contours like I was pretty
    beautiful even
and that maybe my skin was worth being seen

        And worth lust
       sweet reptilian lust

So after realizing a dress
was for special occasions
            and I needed new things
   for the everyday of my new life
      I shaved my legs to stubble
  with an electric razor
and set out for a thrift store

I wasn't frightened
by the long stares and snickers
      because I never imagined
   I'd find so many elated strangers
it was like they knew it was a new day for me
      that I had emerged
from a vegetative sense of self
    to find savage curiosity and confidence

When I made it to the store
(oh sweet transcendence)
    the excess of exciting possibilities
  for a future I'd fully expected to spend
      wearing the kind of t-shirts
        you buy in bulk
would have paralyzed me if I wasn't too busy
      prancing around in skirts
fishnet stockings and pastel tank tops

Who could have known
        how great it is to have a purse?
              I finally allowed myself
        the pink and black plaid shoes
I'd wanted since high-school

        I bought the kind of clothes
I'd always liked seeing on the floor
      next to me and my girlfriend's bed
and that fascination of mine
          suddenly made so much sense
      no wonder women
seemed like the stronger sex
          when I idolized the likes of
L7 Joan Jett Sleater-Kinney and Bikini Kill
    I mean

Rebel girls
    you're the queens of my world
and I do wanna wanna take you home
        so I can try and your clothes
    (duh)

Home I went
    taking every opportunity
  and detour to be seen
    finally snug in my own skin
the breeze catching my hems
        like the sails of a warship
returning to peace in the place they belonged

I haven't stopped since
        even after my parents
stopped talking to me

    even after my girlfriend flipped out
and moved out on me
      life is just too short for sneaking
and hiding and lying
   and languishing alone with a secret self
no one ever meets

   I had to make new friends
and form a new family
       but that first day
when I finally found myself at twenty-four
     a vibrant colossus
of a cross-dressing gender queer
    that's when I started counting my age
       as a person

no longer a prisoner of a gender
        I'd never really been

11.5.86

                Congratulations;
         you're reading yet another
                      poo-painting swan song
from your resident skirt wearing psychopath
       as they try to drink themselves to death
             or at least summon the ghost
      of some anonymous soldier
from the homicidal buskers whisky rebellion

            You see,
       in the political quagmire
             that arose from the ashes of
Richard Nixon's presidency —
       when push-overs reeking of patchouli
hijacked the revolution
                and the hippies grew too weary
       and old and burned out
       to mobilize against the lucrative
             shanghaiing of their progeny —

                the only existential question left
                    isn't so much

IF

                    you should kill yourself

            but what to wear
                  and whether a heroin
overdose in a rowboat straddling a drainage ditch
will send the right message to plebeian traditionalists
                who have to ask

WHY.

Mass murder wouldn't be so unbecoming
        if it wasn't for the media coverage
which means that any decent person
        knows not to leave a note
or make a mess
        unless they really
want their friends and neighbors
        to become daytime television freak-shows
        trying to explain
the carnage
        they didn't have the
common courtesy to clean up
        or at least not call attention to.

        There are rules,
        damn't;
the unpleasant reality
        of a society
obsessed with poking and sniffing
        but never acknowledging
their own feces

So if you're searching for the nirvana of
        not having to live
        in such an
unfortunate trough of human failure
        I beg you,
        utilize proper sanitation
        in such a way that
suggests severe schizophrenia
        paying special care to
include an assortment of details

           that both confounds explanation
          and discourages further examination
while it pays homage to the phenomena
           that leads overly self aware adolescents
                     to torture small animals
                and excel in standardized tests.

       If however
               like your humble author,
           you treat gratuitous solitary day drinking
like some kind of fire-drill
               do not communicate the elation
           of discovering nihilistic bibliophiles'
favorite obsession

                              because
                after all
          if you had any social skills
          you'd know that palatable opinions
                     are not formed,
          but compiled from hours of sound-bites
contingent upon the immediate predicament
                of those you're soliciting
                    and if you'd just
                          spend $19.95
          plus shipping and handling already
               you wouldn't be so depressed
                    about the fact that

       Santa Claus
                     Jesus Christ
                          and Democracy
                     are just illusions

your mother is not so secretly ashamed of you

and the only true achievement
is accepting that without
strict adherence
to the social contract

they won't be willing to call you a success

no matter how satisfied you may be.

32-Ounce Gatorade Bottles
Are A Lady-Man's Best Friend

I had to piss real bad
        on the mother road
that had been called
        Route 66
but now had a dozen names across eight states
        and I was all fagged out
    tall lean strong and covered in glitter
in a sweater dress and skintight leggings
        spelling out nonsense
and clinging to my ass

    I was in the land of shit kickin' boots
        and secret meetings
    about taking *'murika* back
        for the *master race*

But dammit I had to piss
        and that part of Oklahoma
    wasn't exactly bustling with humanity
so I stopped at that gas station
    the first I'd seen in twenty minutes
when I should have been smart enough
    to take any dirt road
        to certain seclusion

On my way in the door it was like
    Edward Snowden showed up
        wearing the ISIS flag as a dress
and walked into Sunday morning service asking

Hey I need to whip my dick out for a minute
        which corner would you prefer I defile?

And I know that the difference was negligible
        at least in their eyes
so I guess I'm to blame
            that the welcoming party
        followed me to the bathroom
and somebody asked me
            why I hadn't cut my dick off yet
        while they were staring at it
cause they wouldn't let me close the door
        lest I decided to do something gay
while standing in their shit closet ankle deep
        in their racist rodeo clown piss

It might have been unnecessary
        but I told them I'd bleed on them
if they didn't let me leave

                and I'm here
                      aren't I?

So that's why you should never drink
        out of anything you find in my car
            If trucker bombs exploded
I could probably take out a small island nation

You SNEAKY Bitch

        Before last night's confessions
            I was completely
       content with being melancholy
in the land of make believe
      chasing exploded stars
           and tacking trinkets to my wall
      and drinking
         and drinking
and defaulting to doing it with you
      for reasons I didn't ever have to explain
           even in every poem I wrote for you

which was every last fucking thing I wrote

        You knew damn well
            the affection that burns
     and bruises
        embolden in my heart
but you brutalized me anyway,
      and breathily told me things
I didn't even realize I wanted to hear

        You saw my whole subtle slide
            into your future
                so don't deny it
           or try to suggest
        that I was just waiting to discover
how much I wanted to respond in kind

     Come to think of it
         you're not to blame

it's all the other spectacular disappointments
              mumbling mouth breathers,
        spineless succubi,
                and FUCKING HIPSTER PUNKS
that have driven me deeper and deeper
        into delighting in this de facto
                effortless muse

        Ya know
                actually
        it's all my own fault

                for not seeing it coming
        and hoping the day would never come
where I'd have to come to grips
        with having no other option

                        in spite of denying
                I rarely had anyone else
                        on my mind

but that doesn't make you any less
        of a sneaky bitch.

Sit On My Face Soulmate

Soulmate please
I need you to sit on my face
so I can tongue-bathe your clit
while you fuck me with your tits
before I bend you over and bang you
in front of my open kitchen window
so the neighbors can hear me
screaming I love you *(oh)*

Oh but judging by your furrowed brow
I must have forgotten
that it's tenderness that turns you on
right?

So let me make you a nice dinner
I promise not to tell you
how amazing your ass looks
I'll just whisper chaste yet inspired love poems
in your ear and I won't try
to kiss your neck or lick your earlobes
I promise
you won't feel my hot breath on your thighs
unless you grab a fist full of my hair
and force my face into your satin slit
like you did this morning

That's EARLIER TODAY SOULMATE!

So don't pretend to be offended
when I tell you I'm throbbing

        and need to taste you
without first taking all three fingers
        out of your pussy
    because I'm confident
in my ability to make you gush
        and whether you like to admit it or not
            you like it rough
        Real respect is giving you what you want
and you want love to leave hand-prints on your ass
            and a salty taste in your mouth

        You show up at my house
            at least once a week unannounced
and promptly get on your knees
            tits and tongue out
        hands in your pants
before you even hit the floor
            You've never heard me complain
            about the semi daily ritual of waking up
                with your delicious hairy sex
hovering over my face

It just needs a few kisses please

        you plead
            and I ALWAYS do
        and you always SCREAM
            your knees like a quivering vice on
my ears until you fall off
            face down ass up

Pound that pussy with your beautiful cock

                you mumble in ecstasy

>   *it's **YOUR** pussy*
> *oh I can't help but give it to you*
>   *please fill it with hot cum*

Yea ...you know damn well
    how much you love savage dick
        and you know damn well
how afterward every time
        after 90 seconds of breathless

> *I'm in love with you*
> *Soulmate*
> *Forever love*
> *Beautiful Muse*
> *Best Friend*
> *Family ...*

you scoop out and rub in
    our mutual orgasm froth
my sewer mouth spewing in your ear
    per your desperate request

I am madly in love with you
    make no mistake about it
so forgive me for feeling like
the best way to show it sometimes
    is giving you so much pleasure
        that your face goes numb
    and that doesn't make you
just a piece of meat
    it means that all the art giggles
adventures and struggles we've shared
        have only made you sexier
So face it
    family
        forever love

IT'S ALL YOUR FAULT

        If you didn't like to fuck me so much
            we'd still just be
                    best friends

Professional Failure

      You gotta wake up
real early in the morning
        to be a
                PROFESSIONAL
                   failure

      something like 4:30 am
and spend 25 minutes punching the snooze alarm
          praying for death
      and absolution of the debt
you are basically killing yourself over

      You gotta consider throwing it all away
          every day
              running into the night
      taking on a fake name
             and living in a van
         in the deserts of (O)Bolivia

      You gotta start collecting your memoirs
a compilation of all the mean things you say to yourself
          and the lists
      of all the jobs you got fired from
and all the people you fucked

You gotta learn how to play one blues song
(because one blues song will be enough)
to strum as you look at a loaded gun on the table

You gotta eat food that's way past it's prime
      last week's raw bacon like it was candy

        get so low
            you find the much better half
of a chipotle burrito on the sidewalk
        when you're stumbling home drunk
            around 7:45 pm
        and tuck your shirt in
           cause it feels fancy

You gotta have dreams
        you're so scared of
that you hide your whole life away

            You gotta be determined enough
                to stand at the edge
        forever

but so crippled

            you never jump.

In Junk Yard Dogs We Trust

Through all the screaming
        and gnashing of teeth
                on the eve of another
totalitarian regime
                taking power
                      I try to remember
        how it felt to believe
that it was all going to get better
        four years ago
                      a decade ago

I remember getting called a *faggot*
        being blindsided with a fist
and pushed in the snow last year

                I remember my co-worker
        last month saying *lazy n....*
                (you know)
and looking at me with the most sickening smile
        like she thought
                those things crossed my mind

I remember how many times
        I've started a sentence
            I'd like to
        and how few times
that sentence has ended
                show her a safe place
        since birth
and how few times I've spoken up
                when all the talk of sluts
makes me just a little sick to my stomach

I remember what violence tastes like
from both sides

I remember how yesterday
I was standing in line to buy pepper spray
about to head to the rich part of town
to burn some old right-winger's eyes
right out of his fucking skull
like it could make this populist puppet
president of ours not wage wars
in the name of the white man's revenge

I remember
how almost every dog I've ever met
has been scared and confused
and desperate to be loved
but leads with their teeth
because that's what they've been taught to do

That's why we keep up the facade
of electing Leaders

because beneath it all
it not that we don't trust each other
so much as
we know we can't trust ourselves
to stop the cycle

Dead Flowers in Denial

       It was 20 years
two days ago
       that I moved to Kansas City
and since I insist on never calling it home
       I should probably quit putting off
            getting there
       because while it's been wonderful
                   at times
we both know you won't be here either
       this time next year

           I've never found solid ground
       and you have been waiting to fly
since we saw each other
       already inseparable strangers
           at first crash

I've been juggling hornets' nests
       trying to find north
                and you have scouted
            your next dozen landing places
I am still struggling to kill the worm
              all by myself
       but you have taken up farming
       because while we are both starving
           we are also opposite directions
           in a tightening nest
       who keep deciding to stick around
because we've never stayed gone

                    That soon turns us into dead flowers
                                in denial
                    chargeless prisoners
                            inviting the beheading

It makes us forget how last year ended
            even if that inevitability means
our shattered dreams
                    about this very cruel place

            It makes the object of all our prayers

                            death

even if that inevitability means
our shattered dreams
about promises

Long Island Sound

It's not easy
        telling sixty-five-million people
across twelve states
        that you just can't take it anymore
and you're taking off

        So I start off nice and soft and sweet
the way they need their news in the Midwest

I give them the old line
        (and it's true)
                 It's me
        not you
        and it's not right to make you suffer
            the tragic top volume vitriol
    of my lawnmower-blade-tongue anymore
        so I'm gonna leave
            and go back east
        where people can take the truth
        without a spoonful of sugar first

The whole being nice thing
            doesn't work out so well
      it never has
and my sarcasm is about as subtle as skywriting
        there is no hiding how goddamn sick
I am of those spineless bible-thumping
butt-hurt little babies
        but it's not my fault
            I just wasn't raised right

      I grew up in a place
where kindness often took the form of
      Look you little bastard
if you weren't so wonderful
      and beautiful and hilarious
there's no way I'd put up
      with all this shit from you

      But ya know what?
that made it real easy
      to figure out who your friends were
cause they were the ones busting your balls everyday
      and loyal to you regardless
of what anybody ever had to say
      they saw through you to the soul
and they could recognize your stupid smiling face
      several crowded city blocks away
      and they would come running
and yelling to embrace you on both cheeks
      before punching you in the ribs

      Make no mistake about it
      none of them were friendly
      but they made great friends

And you showed your affection for each other
by screaming about anything and everything
      you cared about
      and sometimes you did agree
      but most of the time
      you wrestled about what was real
      you argued about a better tomorrow
and everybody knew they were better for it

      It's true that I'm broken
because all my friends are beautiful assholes

and I think the kindest thing you can call a woman
                is a *tough bitch*
cause it means she's fearless
        and resiliant and takes care of her own

        My aunts refer to their husbands as
that ugly worthless fat slob over there
even as it's the farthest thing from the truth
even when they are the best friends they've ever had
My uncles are SAINTS that love their wives like sunlight
        but everybody likes to laugh about it
                because they understand irony
        and savage commitment

So I'm sorry
        but I equate being made fun of with belonging
        and empty compliments with contempt
so when I gotta pocket fulla change
                and strong opinions
        charity is always sharing my two cents
no matter who's fragile fucking feelings get hurt

        And maybe that's the problem
I wasn't raised right
        for the razor's edge of midwestern polite
where treating people the way I'd want to be
makes me an abusive asshole lowlife
        which obviously wouldn't matter so much
if it wasn't all such a colossal misunderstanding

        So anyway
                I might be stupid
but I'm not insane

       so I'm moving back to where
my friends will greet me

       Good Morning Motherfucker
and I will know instantly that it means

yo bro bro
       I love you like family

Shit-Brains Soup

       I used to be afraid of heights
until getting all alone
            and climbing as high as I could
just to look down and see myself splattered
            unexpected concrete soup crater
               all alone
became peace and safety

       Some time between my teenaged self
fighting mortality and becoming
       a busted up twenty something
           with real bad luck
       I went from fearing I'd never be loved
and run out of time
       to being more scared of surviving
            than anything
so I drove blind straight through intersections
       secretly hoping my shattered body
           would be the final resting place
for a semi-trailers jackknife
       and I started taking horizon pictures
           from roof tops
       with sick pleasure in the doublespeak
of showing them off
           like I wanted to be soaring
       when I'd just figured out
that falling feels like flying
              for a little while

 I was making plans
           to make the best of things

    make damn sure the best things
       were the last things
     and that I didn't have to suffer
surviving the inevitable crash

    It was a lot easier being young
       and full of hurt
     I could cheer myself up hoping
but now the most dangerous days
     are the ones where things seem
   to be looking up

       because then I start looking up …

I wanted to kill myself much worse
     on my wedding day
   then I did when I found out
     they didn't love me anymore
   and when I think about driving
      my car off a bridge
   into the freezing river
     it's probably because
I've found something new to love
   and better me than my memories of it
to drown in a world of shit

I think they call that fatalism
   and god I know it's stupid
     but what's really sick
is having a head that spins things
      so that I see sex in *Guernica*
     and carnage
in any attempt to show me kindness

What's sad
        is being so used to being sad
that I stop on the roofs of parking garages
        on the way to friend's house's
because I have no faith I'll have any fun

        It's every day
                      without exception
        a frightened flightless bird
with an instinctual imperative to be airborne
                who knows they'll sink
like solid steel in quicksand
            but still can't stop themselves
        from looking out into the chasm

        And I can't explain how I'm still alive
                besides the fact
        that I keep my feet on the ground
and I'm not afraid of heights anymore
            because the worst case scenario
        is that I'll keep feeling this way
                    not that one day
        I might jump

If Love

Incarnations of chrysanthemums
        are buried beneath
the Midwest's December ice-sheets
screaming for sunlight to come save them
        but they are stuck
sedentary seeds trapped by the thin yet
impenetrable divide of seasons

Starlight sneaks through the soil
        and excites the root systems
with dreams preparing for photosynthesis
        and speculations about thirsty veins
sucking on hard packed snow

        Above ground everybody already says
it's gonna be too cold for the groundhog
        and no matter the genocide
of the neighbor boy's basketball
        or bunny rabbits who only
                like to shit out pretty things
the flowers will seduce bees
                to steal their pollen
        and I will come outside
after another long winter of sweating
        paranoid that my space heater will fail
and my pipes will freeze
                on May first
with coffee too scalding to drink
        warming my hands
and assuaging those fears
        that I won't soon feel warm

       I will come up on a chrysanthemum
proof I've made it through
              another season of darkness
       and so too has all the precarious life
I look to for hope

       And I will sip deep
upon the first buds of spring
       before walking back inside
             with a chest full of hot air
hot enough to be ready for my coffee
            and another year

       And as that bee
                  slips down my throat
            and stings
                  I will shuffle back inside
coughing and chugging coffee
        to a bed that had bet the farm
            on befriending a new woman
        but instead
I will be suffocating and staring out the window
        at a lost dog on the sidewalk
            and I will be saying
                  with the rest of the world
       too worn out to survive a new season

       if love ...

       without enough time to figure out
what might have been

                  but only the peace
            of really wanting to

Only In Dreams Wet
With Ferlinghetti's Sweat

                I'm wishing for a dive diner
                        in a old time train car
        with nothing but a long counter
           and some corner space
    to congregate around black coffee
the kind of place hobo's spend their change
    on Reuben sandwiches
and day laborers can drift into
           with two dollars
      and leave with mustard breath
                and full bellies
The waitresses should be enthusiastic
ambassadors to swashbuckling symposiums
                by keeping the cups full
         and the kitchen open
  and the newspapers numerous
    and all the area's sleepless sages singing
Those stewards should be young
                but experienced
          raven-haired and green-eyed
epiphany pilgrims lusting for sweat so bad
            they find themselves practicing
      retelling all of human history
           in the space of sparse syllables
    to virtually anyone who will listen
I pray that fire hazard of fancies
           would be a four am hangout
      for the poets and strays
          the addicts

                the freaks
                                the faggots
                the beautiful souls running away
from ugly pasts
                        and the past lovers
meeting for clandestine mornings
                        the churchgoers won't be shy
                but neither will the drag queens
                                as they rub elbows
                and sit down only several feet away
to discuss their passions unashamed
        there will be five languages spoken
between the fire code capacity crowd
                of eighteen
all shouting a thousand syncopations a second
                        with salacious smiles
cross-referencing their table cloth crayon maps
        of the last million miles
across the country and around the block
                praying for peace and prosperity
                bleeding and breaking bones
                                to bludgeon alarm clocks
                all listening with genuine gratefulness
                        for getting to hear
the lessons accidental prophets rode in on
                not a soul would forget
        the common ground
                they all diverged from
and were unafraid to return to
        and no one would ask for a poem
                cause they'd know well enough
to already be hearing one

Shining Time Space Station

      Our problems might feel real
but who says our solutions
      have to be reasonable?!

      I vote to turn our delusions
         into delightful things!

So stop being scared
      my Spanish steel
      has cut through the knot of snakes
surrounding your bed fortress
         so now it's safe for secrets
      and the witchcraft that makes us
         SUPERHEROES!
    wonder twins who
create a whole new world of wonder
      whether anyone else sees it or not

      Some people will call us crazy
    for dressing up like panda bears
but they're just jealous of our super powers
    like you are a master of disguises
      and ventriloquist tricks
         you can escape any trap
    and my mind can make
    sunshine rainbows and cotton candy
the sole conception of any would be killer

      Every monster is our friend!

No matter what peril our adventures find us in
      remember this constant fear won't be fatal
         so long as one of us
is always Sancho Panza
        to the other's PTSD OCD
Borderline Bi-Polar Psychotic Quixote
    then those windmills won't stand a chance!

When you tell me all the bones are broken
     inside your body I will remind you
        that I'm a psychic
as well as a surgeon
       so I can see though your skin
       and it seems all you need is sunlight

    When I get weak
        and start seeing my own death
at every intersection
      you will sing Elvis's Christmas songs
        until we lift off the ground
          like Santa's sled
     and soar above every
        semi plowing through stop signs

    When your insomnia
leads you to see assassins
      and feeds an obsession with chivalry
        I will be your *Dulcinea*
      and by practicing saving me
        we can learn to save ourselves

      And saving
saving can be as simple
       as realizing that too much sanity
    might be madness

                        and maddest of all might be
seeing the world as it is
                and not as it should be

So when the machines
        inside our skin malfunction
                and our cell phones pick up
secret government transmissions
        we only need to take out
our dollar store magic wands and wave them
        while we watch
                        our terrors wash away
        like a paper-mache goblin
                        we've thrown water on
                we can don our tinfoil hats
        hiding from the aliens
                and the secret police
        under the force-field of our fancies
                where sadness isn't real
but the magical thinking of mania is
        where no one can tell us we can't fly
                and talk to animals
                        and turn invisible
        so that the bad things can't find us
                        and even if they do
        no one can tell us we can't ride
sunflowers into the sky
                where we are always safe

I Guess I'll Never Learn

My first job taught me that pretending to be Jewish
    isn't such a solid long term strategy
and my second job that adults will abuse children
    in any way they can get away with

    On my third job
        I discovered that
    even if you have warrants
the police aren't always showing up to see you
    sometimes they just want a sandwich

            My fourth job taught me
that calling your coworkers *spaghetti faggots* —
    even if it's an inside joke
and you're a cross-dresser —
    is rarely advisable in front of the owners
        Mister and Mister Pellerito

My fifth job taught me not to eat acid and come to work
    My sixth job to check the schedule
        My seventh that I'm a coward
My eighth that just because
    I've started working doesn't mean
that the drug screen came back clean

My ninth job taught me that
    when you work for the government
  the less work you do the better they like you
    I pretended to be looking for someone
very important they've never heard of
        for at least four hours a day

and after that I ended up working job ten
        for eight months where I learned how
to rob the register blind and cover my tracks

        Job eleven taught me that masturbating
                in the supply closet
isn't all it's cracked up to be

Jobs twelve and thirteen were pleasant really
                and not worth mentioning

        Job fourteen taught me that dreadlocks
                will make you the fall guy
anytime anyone gets high in a two block radius
        Job fifteen that
yo no puedo hablar español (es verdad)

        Job sixteen taught me that if you
drink a fifth of gin than you will
                sweat juniper poison for days
        Job seventeen that smoking meth
makes you a *better* employee
        because clean floors and walls
and mop-sinks and TRASHCANS
                are more important than profits

                Job eighteen taught me that
        when your boss is fucking half the staff
          you better be extra nice to everyone
             just in case your arch nemesis
          suddenly becomes the latest notch
                    on his bedpost

Job nineteen taught me how to spot a pyramid scheme

Job twenty that I sell cars like old people fuck
          and that used car salesmen really are
                  the lowest form of life on earth
          Jobs twenty-one through twenty-four
taught me that nobody who ran through a jungle
          to escape certain death
has any sympanthy for my white boy problems

          Job twenty-five that actually,
                no one does

          Job twenty-six taught me that it is possible
to get a job at MacDonald when I'm black out drunk
          I don't remember filling out the application
                or showing up for the interview
          I just remember them calling and asking
    why I was two hours late for my first shift
and I remember telling them

BECUASE SUCKING DICK AT A TRUCK STOP
       SEEMED LIKE A MORE DIGNIFIED WAY
  TO MAKE A LIVING

Job twenty-seven taught me that dreams
                do come true
                but that they don't last
if my big mouth has anything to do with it

All I've actually learned
                is that

        I'll never learn

and that if you're gonna be dumb
                you better be
                              tough

Big Strong Man

    Whoa
               I see what you've been saying
about crawling on your belly for stability

               Now that I'm unemployed
my paranoia too
            has been leading me
       to petition like a parasite
            for the salvation of security
and swear off my obscenities and sparkle

               I haven't worn woman's clothes
since I got the news
       and was sent out to starve

I get the feeling I'm straight out of second chances
                    screwed like wild swine
             waiting for the slaughter

So I've stopped drinking and dreaming of greatness
I've sunk into the market of sub-skilled laborers
       sucking on the tit of sympathy
           and even there
I'm cramped by my capabilities
       censored to the lowest forms of servitude

My bravado has been flattened
                  now that I'm floating
           on barely enough money to pay the bills
               and I consider
           collapsing on the church-steps

        crying out for mercy
to a god I'm conveniently believing in again

    I'm just a profane sinner

    I'll say,

    But with Jesus
now that I'm sorry
    I can be forgiven
and find a good job
    and a wife
and father nine children
    (not necessarily in that order)
and I will never again feel defeated
    because piety
    doesn't provoke these kinds of
    emergencies

Yes, I'm putting on a tie,
and turning my life around
        THIS MOMENT

I'm taking the sound advice
and silencing all impulses to stray

because from here on out
I'm gonna be...
        a big strong man

Drunk Driving Is NOT An Extreme Sport

The nature of shame
is that you want to stop
    or wish you wouldn't have
but know you just can't help yourself

and I have this habit
of facefucking myself with alcohol
    anytime I got a long drive ahead of me

Kids
    please realize that it isn't cool
to be driving down the highway
    doing like a hundred
        weaving between lanes
    cause suddenly you are convinced
        getting to the next detour
has the same consequences as *Cannonball Run*
    and maybe that Corvette in the left lane
has three times the engine as your 97 camry
        but you are at least 10 times crazier
        and you'll crash
    passing on the shoulder
        if that's what it takes
to reach the pot'o'gold first

Last weekend wasn't the first time
        this year
    that I got home
and didn't remember anything past

                    pissing myself in a gas station

          this time I was knock-kneed
and pinching my dick like a sad six year old
                    and everybody was watching me
          as I tried to shuffle outside
                    but ended up slipping
          on the trail of used beer I leaving

                    I got up gunza' blazing
flinging potato chips as subeterfuge
                              cover fire
                    as I crawled to the front door
          hopped in my car and drove into traffic
with my driver door still hanging open
                    laying on the horn
deciding this was a bonny and clyde situation
     and red
               or even red and blue
          shouldn't mean stop

          Waking up in the passenger seat
and the search for my keys on the front lawn
                    is a routine I always regret
                         having to go through
     again

                         Kids
                    it's not cool
          having no idea where you've been
                    or how you managed to escape

I laugh at so many other near misses

but swerving till I wake up to the sound
               of the rumble strips on the shoulder
       always fills me with the dread
               of being lost
         and hoping I'm not the source
of anyone's loss

I just don't REMEMBER
       hurting no body

               or where all the dents came from
                   for that matter

It's easy for me to say it'll never happen again
       until I'm already drunk
             distracted
racing a train across the tracks
        and horny

       It always starts almost innocently —
           the shimmering lights
     of a city I've never seen
on a highway that's been dark for hours
          I tell myself
       I'll have a beer and burger
but
               I have the beer first
         so it turns into 3 bourbons
            and then I get on my phone
and start planning my next stop

           Just an hour down the road!
         It only adds 20 minutes to my trip!

     Then I'm drunk
             and every bright light in bumfuck
                   means more alcohol
so I stop and pick up a six pack
                 at the Kum and Go
         Jizz and Jett
             Break and Beat
     gas station

I always claim I won't drink them
                while driving
        after the first one
till I get home later
               cause it's late already
and I just need 3 more nightcaps

     you know how that always works out...

        Kids
             drunk driving
   isn't an extreme sport

cause the only prize is surviving

     and the only guarantee

        is that you will fail the fuck
out of the drug test

A Love Poem Not Quite About Jason Ryberg

You taught me
about kissing cat piss stained poetry books
                and reading them real loud
    in the middle of the night naked
in my bathroom hoping someone would hear
         so my life wouldn't be changing alone
      and when my echoes weren't answered
it taught me about the sadness and abandon both
                of finding home in a place
      no one else loved

        We met on that street corner in front
of the bookstore for months after work
      every night until we sanctified it
considered the stories we passed
    back and forth our scriptures
and confused ourselves into thinking
              it was the place we belonged
    I wanted you to belong to me
in ways that were too urgent to keep quiet
          but too serious
to keep a straight face about
      so how I felt about you became a joke
no one thought was funny
         because it hurts to watch people make
      the same mistakes over and over
while they make promises about
      what their heart-crossed futures hold

                You and me met pissing into the wind
                            almost too glad to cross streams
and have someone else's filth in our faces
                            We needed heroes
                        who were neither very old
                                    nor very pretty

If it wasn't for you
            I might have crawled back to academia
and let them teach me about satisfying stipulations
            instead I'll keep trying to please myself
            knowing now from experience
that you're just like me
                    so there's no pleasing you either

but I guess it's better that way
            if it means we'll be forced to keep trying
harder and harder to be happy
                    maybe even together

Murphy's Eulogy: As Dictated

When the hepatic coma comes & I can't tell
the difference between shitting and shivering
           just throw me in a pine box
      that you make yourself
                    as I writhe on the floor
Build it with wet wood
      stolen from a lumber graveyard
& string it together with catgut twine and tar
      When my face turns blue
          and my lips gray
throw me in that pine box
face down and drown me in dry ice
                You nail the lid on
      and pretend the wisps of smoke
are the escaping soul
           of a self I never believed in
      Pull up a few chairs to my box
and set your whiskey down on top of me
and suck it down till you can't remember
           all the secrets I let slip
      and screw on top of me
so we can be that close one last time
               Then in the morning
after you've woken up and washed away
          what's left of me on you
      take that pine box
like it was six-months-worth of coyote shit
from the chicken coop to the highway
& throw me off the bridge
      and into the river to Alphabet City

Powers Whiskey

       I've tried to put you down
and I'll be damned if you don't keep coming back
            like the bad habit you are
after a few weeks

   and after a few more weeks
              we're out in the open again
        and no one believes I ever stayed away
even as long as I did

       It happens in the winter
after I've scared everyone away
            and I'm alone and cold
              and almost but not quite contrite
        and it happens in the spring too
where everyone is looking for something new
         and you and me are just in the same place
we've always been but it's time to shake the dust
               and you and me get lost
     in the shuffle of transformations

       I can't stay away from you too long though
so I start skipping out on friends I'm only making
and making up excuses for why I'm gone
            I tell myself the screaming
   and the psychoshitstorm is just that part of me
that wants to get out struggling to find traction

      I say *It's good for me to be crazy like this*
cause I ain't got no home but chaos
        I can't admit to myself that I'm just bad

and maybe you're bad for me
        but all I see from my perch in the corner
is how well it's working out for everyone around you

You're making easier the impossible hopes
        on the tips of everyone's tongues
but I'm always on the verge of tipping over
I guess what I'm trying to say is that I love you
        because I'll never see you as the problem
and I don't feel like I can fix the problems
                that make us catastrophic

        Even now I've fallen over and got back up
and as soon as I'm stable again my first thought
        is to scoop you up and bring you to my lips
            like it's gonna be different cause
        I got halfway through hell
and that's as far as I've ever made it anyway
            and since I can remember
        you were always there to greet me

        It's not that I never hoped you'd stay gone
more like you were all the places I ever wanted to be
            I know there was life before you
but the blur you've made
                hand to mouth
                horror and fallout
brings me back to when I didn't know any better
and I was the trash in a dumpster fire

        Every day I make a list of things to do
and moving on stays at the top of my list
            but the one thing I just won't

            I just wont

ever bother to finish

Ezhno's Confirmation Name:
Francis (Of Assisi)

St Francis grew up rich but found his home among beggars, one day giving away all he had to someone his father described as a gutter punk scum fuck. Lots of people mocked him or ignored him, so he just talked to the birds, calling all the creatures 'brother' 'sister' and later, after a divine revelation, the genderless 'family.' He embraced what the other saints were afraid of, and, when he came upon a village tortured by their fear of the neighborhood wolf, tracked down the wolf and became his friend, too. Turns out the wolf was just a broke blues man with one hell of a howl...*just 300 pounds of love and joy*, and Francis saw what no one else did. Francis happened to know how to play piano (every rich prick plays piano), so he joined the wolf out on the road, playing the blues and preaching the gospel that everyone has the capacity to be beautiful and holy, even as we are all basically just beasts.

Francis is the Patron Saint of Animals and Ecology

www.ingramcontent.com/pod-product-compliance
Lightning Source LLC
Chambersburg PA
CBHW020621300426
44113CB00007B/728